PELÉ

SOCCER HERO

PERCY LEED

LERNER PUBLICATIONS ◆ MINNEAPOLIS

SCORE BIG with sports fans, reluctant readers, and report writers!

Lerner™ Sports is a database profiling today's most popular sports stars! Introduce students to digital research skills through high-interest sports content, including soccer, hockey, football, baseball, basketball, and more. Hundreds of photos, thousands of bite-sized facts, and timely tie-ins to championship games make Lerner Sports the perfect bridge from the playing field to the library.

LERNER SPORTS FEATURES:

☑ Keyword search
☑ Topic navigation menus
☑ Fast facts
☑ Related bio suggestions to encourage more reading
☑ Admin view of reader statistics
☑ Fresh content updated regularly
and more!

Visit LernerSports.com for a free trial!

Lerner Publications Company
An imprint of Lerner Publishing Group, Inc.
241 First Avenue North
Minneapolis, MN 55401 USA

For reading levels and more information, look up this title at www.lernerbooks.com.

Main body text set in Myriad Pro Semibold.
Typeface provided by Adobe.

Designer: Mary Ross **Photo Editor:** Brianna Kaiser

Library of Congress Cataloging-in-Publication Data

Names: Leed, Percy, 1968– author.
Title: Pelé : soccer hero / Percy Leed.
Description: Minneapolis : Lerner Publications, 2022. | Series: Epic sports bios | Includes bibliographical references and index. | Audience: Ages 7–11 | Audience: Grades 2–3 | Summary: "During his soccer career, superstar forward Pelé won three FIFA World Cup titles and became the all-time leading scorer for Brazil. Find out more about his record-breaking achievements and lasting legacy in this biography"— Provided by publisher.
Identifiers: LCCN 2021000257 (print) | LCCN 2021000258 (ebook) | ISBN 9781728404318 (library binding) | ISBN 9781728420493 (paperback) | ISBN 9781728418094 (ebook)
Subjects: LCSH: Pelé, 1940—-Juvenile literature. | Soccer players—Brazil—Biography—Juvenile literature.
Classification: LCC GV942.7.P42 L44 2022 (print) | LCC GV942.7.P42 (ebook) | DDC 796.334092 [B]—dc23

LC record available at https://lccn.loc.gov/2021000257
LC ebook record available at https://lccn.loc.gov/2021000258

Manufactured in the United States of America
1-48489-49003-2/11/2021

TABLE OF CONTENTS

CHALLENGE FOR THE CUP

As a 17-year-old playing in the 1958 World Cup, Pelé had a lot to prove. He had only started his pro soccer career a year before. In the knockout round, Pelé and the Brazilians were well matched against Wales. Neither team could score, until Pelé got the ball. He scored the only goal of the game, giving Brazil a 1–0 win.

Pelé chases the ball to the net in1958

FACTS AT A GLANCE

Date of birth: October 23, 1940

Position: forward, midfielder

League: Brazil national team, Série A, North American Soccer League (NASL)

Professional highlights: led his pro league in goals in his first season; won three World Cups; scored 1,281 career goals

Personal highlights: son of a pro soccer player, Dondinho; named a national treasure of Brazil; named FIFA's Co-Player of the Century

In a match against France, Pelé did something amazing. He scored his first hat trick and gave Brazil the advantage they needed to win the game 5–2. Brazil headed to the final against Sweden, their toughest competition yet.

Pelé fights for control of the ball.

Pelé (*center*) cries after winning his first World Cup.

A high ball came at Pelé. He hit it with his chest and then kicked the ball into the net. Goal! With the game winding down, Brazil was winning 4–2. But Pelé kept fighting and scored a last-minute goal. He and Brazil had claimed the World Cup!

STARTING WITH SANTOS

Edson Arantes do Nascimento was born on October 23, 1940, in Tres Coracoes, Brazil, to Joao Ramos do Nascimento and Celeste Arantes. When Edson was born, his father looked at him and said, "This one will be a great soccer player."

Pelé's hometown of Tres Coracoes, Brazil

BECOMING PELÉ

How Pelé got his name or who gave it to him remains a mystery—even to him. At first, Pelé hated the name. He'd even get into fights with other kids over it. "I must have lost most of [the fights]," he said, "because the name stuck!"

Nicknames are common in Brazilian soccer. Edson's father was known as Dondinho. Dondinho played for several teams, including the Bauru Athletic Club (BAC). Edson played for the youth team, Little BAC. People called him Pelé. The Little BAC coach was Waldemar de Brito, who played in the 1934 World Cup.

In 1955, de Brito said that Pelé was ready to play pro soccer. He also knew the owner of the pro team Santos. Pelé, 15, headed to Sao Paulo, Brazil, to try out for Santos. He thought he would be practicing with those in his age group and was shocked to learn he'd play with the team's top players.

Pelé's incredible play with Santos gained him national attention and a place on Brazil's World Cup team.

Two other talented players were trying out for the same spot on the team. Pelé's chances were slim. But that changed with a practice game.

Pelé started the game on the bench and ran onto the field as a replacement. By the end of the game, he had scored four of the team's six goals. He showed he was a determined midfielder. In his first season, he led the league in goals and earned his spot on Brazil's national team.

LOSING OUT ON A WIN

Since Brazil had won the 1958 World Cup, they automatically qualified for the 1962 tournament. But they scheduled practice games to stay fresh. They took on Portugal and won. After the game, Pelé felt a pain in his leg. In the next three games, he scored four goals despite his injury.

Pelé dives to gain control of the ball.

Pelé (*left*) dribbles down the field.

Three days later, Pelé took the field against Czechoslovakia. He and Brazil needed to win or tie if they wanted to advance to the next round. Pelé got the ball and dribbled past defenders. When he neared the goal, he kicked the ball. It hit the post and bounced right back to him.

This time, Pelé kicked harder. Pain shot through his leg, and he fell to the ground. At the time, teams weren't allowed substitutes. Not wanting to let his team down, he gritted his teeth and continued. The game ended in a 0–0 tie. But Pelé's injury persisted. He was sidelined as Brazil beat England, Chile, and Czechoslovakia to take home the 1962 World Cup.

NATIONAL TREASURE

After winning the 1958 World Cup, Pelé gained international attention. European clubs wanted him on their teams and offered him a lot of money. But Brazil didn't want to give up their superstar player. So the country's president declared Pelé a national treasure and blocked him from playing for teams based in other countries. The ban lasted 10 years.

PUSHING FORWARD

Two months after his injury, Pelé got a confidence boost. In August 1962, Santos was playing in the Libertadores Cup in Argentina. The winner would be the champion of South America. Santos made the finals, and Pelé scored two goals to help his team win 3–0. Against Benfica, a Portuguese club, he scored two goals. The teams played

Pelé celebrates after Brazil claimed the 1962 World Cup.

Pelé (*first row, second from right*) poses with some of his teammates at the 1966 World Cup.

again, this time in Portugal. Just minutes into the game, Pelé scored. Then he scored two more times. In the second half, he added an assist and two more goals.

Pelé had prepared for four years for the 1966 World Cup in England. But 40 players were selected for the team and were divided into several groups. Pelé thought this was a mistake. How could the players get to know one another if they weren't playing together?

Pelé races to the action as a goalie catches the ball in 1966.

Brazil overcame their challenges and beat Bulgaria 2–0. They weren't as lucky against Hungary, losing 3–1. The two-time World Cup champions needed a miracle to make the second round. They would have to beat Portugal. From the start, the game was a disaster. After 24 minutes, Portugal was winning 2–0. Brazil rallied for one goal, but it wasn't enough to win the game. Portugal won 3–1, and Brazil was out of the tournament.

After the disappointing performance, Pelé and Brazil were ready to reclaim the World Cup in Mexico in 1970. Brazil won all six of its games leading into the tournament. Pelé was on fire, scoring six goals in six games. The team's situation was much different from that of the 1966 team. "We understood each other perfectly," Pelé said. "I think that is what gave us a great advantage."

Pelé leaps backward to head the ball in a 1970 World Cup match.

On June 3, 1970, Brazil began its quest for a third World Cup in a game against Czechoslovakia. Brazil's bad memories of 1966 returned when the Czechs took an early 1–0 lead. Brazil tied the game 10 minutes later. In the second half, Pelé trapped a pass with his chest. Then he kicked the ball into the net. Brazil scored two more goals for a 4–1 win.

Pelé and Brazil made it to the final against Italy. Italy had a great defense, but Pelé cracked it. When the ball sailed to him, he knocked it into the net with his head. Goal! Brazil's Clodoaldo made a bad pass near his team's goal. Italy made him pay for the mistake by scoring a goal to tie the game.

Pelé raises his arms to celebrate a Brazil goal against Italy.

Teammates carry Pelé on their shoulders after winning the 1970 World Cup.

But Brazil didn't give up. They scored three more times, with Pelé assisting two of them. Brazil had won its third World Cup! "I felt as though I had achieved everything I set out to achieve," Pelé said.

In 1972, Pelé and Santos played games all over the world. He played his 1,000th game for Santos in Paramaribo, Suriname. His years playing soccer were catching up with him. But he wasn't ready to let go until 1974, when he announced his retirement.

Pelé waves to the crowd after his final game with Santos.

Pelé's last game for Santos was against the Sao Paulo team, Ponte Preta. Nothing out of the ordinary happened until 20 minutes into the game, when Pelé caught a pass—with his hands! The other players stopped. The crowd went silent. Pelé ran to the center circle and dropped to his knees. He lifted his arms and turned to face each corner of the stadium. Fans rose to their feet and cheered.

BRINGING SOCCER TO THE STATES

After Pelé's last game, Clive Toye called him. Toye ran a pro soccer team in New York and wanted to see if Pelé would play for them. Pelé had the opportunity to bring his love of soccer to the US. He accepted Toye's offer.

Pelé dodges defenders in 1975.

On June 11, 1975, the New York Cosmos introduced Pelé as their newest player. In Pelé's first game with the Cosmos, they beat Dallas. But the rest of the 1975 season was a struggle. The Cosmos finished 10–12 and didn't make the playoffs. "It was clear there was a lot of work to be done," Pelé said.

Pelé playing his first game with the Cosmos

Pelé runs hard to beat two defenders to the ball.

With the regular season over, the Cosmos flew to Europe and the Caribbean to play games. The team had its ups and downs, but the more the members played together, the better they became.

The 1976 season was Pelé's first full season with the Cosmos. In the first eight games, they had a 4–4 record. Pelé and the team worked hard and improved their record to 11–5, good enough for the playoffs.

The team picked up wins against the Washington Diplomats and the Tampa Bay Rowdies. Attendance at games kept rising, and they were regularly shown on television. Kids all across the US joined soccer leagues. Pelé made a lot of people in the US fall in love with soccer, but he had one goal left to accomplish. He wanted a league championship.

Pelé meets with young soccer players in 1975.

Pelé holds the league championship trophy high above his head.

In August 1977, a crowd of 35,000 filled Civic Stadium in Portland, Oregon, to see the champion match between the Cosmos and the Seattle Sounders. The Cosmos scored first, but Seattle quickly tied the game. Neither team could pull ahead, until Cosmos player Chinaglia scored a header. Time ran out, and the Cosmos became champions! The team carried Pelé off the field in triumph.

The last team Pelé played for before retiring was his beloved Santos. In a special game between the Cosmos and Santos, Pelé played a half for each team. He started with the Cosmos and curved a free kick into the net from 30 yards out. At halftime, Pelé pulled on his Santos uniform. He tried to score, but the Cosmos stopped their star player. When the game ended, players from both teams ran out and hugged Pelé.

Pelé competes in his final pro soccer match.

Fans celebrate Pelé and his lasting impact on soccer.

Pelé ended his soccer career with a stunning 1,280 goals in 1,367 games. In 1999, FIFA named both him and Argentina's Diego Maradona the Co-Player of the Century. Many people from around the world fell in love with soccer and its hero, Pelé.

SIGNIFICANT STATS

Won six Brazilian championships

Was the top scorer at the Intercontinental Cup twice and won the cup twice

Won three World Cups

Won a league championship with the New York Cosmos

Won the Libertadores Cup twice and once was the cup's top scorer

GLOSSARY

assist: a pass from a teammate that leads directly to a goal

dribble: move the soccer ball up the field using one's feet

FIFA: a group that oversees soccer around the world

final: the championship game of a tournament

hat trick: three goals scored in a game by one person

header: a shot or pass made by hitting the ball with the head

knockout round: the stage of a tournament in which a game's winning team advances to the next round and the losing team is out of the tournament

midfielder: a position in soccer whose main responsibility is covering the middle of the field

pro: short for professional, taking part in an activity to make money

substitute: a soccer player who sits on the bench until being called to replace a player on the field

SOURCE NOTES

8   James S. Haskins, *Pelé: A Biography* (New York: Doubleday, 1976), 39.

9   Harry Harris, *Pelé: His Life and Times* (New York: Welcome Rain, 2001), 14.

17 Pelé. *Pelé: The Autobiography* (London: Simon and Schuster UK, 2008), 197.

19 Haskins, *Pelé: A Biography*, 133.

22 Pelé, *Pelé*, 291.

LEARN MORE

Avise, Jonathan. *Lionel Messi vs. Pelé*. Minneapolis: Sports Zone, 2018.

Biography: Pelé
https://www.biography.com/athlete/pele

Fishman, Jon M. *Soccer's G.O.A.T.: Pelé, Lionel Messi, and More*. Minneapolis: Lerner Publications, 2020.

KidsHealth: Five Ways to Avoid Sports Injuries
https://www.kidshealth.org/en/kids/sport-safety.html?WT.ac=ctg#catfit

Sports Illustrated Kids: Soccer
https://www.sikids.com/tag/soccer

Weakland, Mark. *Soccer Records*. Mankato, MN: Black Rabbit Books, 2021.

INDEX

PHOTO ACKNOWLEDGMENTS

Image credits: AP Photo/Uncredited, p. 4; Todd Strand/Independent Picture Service, pp. 5, 28; Sueddeutsche Zeitung Photo/Alamy Stock Photo, p. 6; AP Photo/WCSCC AP, pp. 7, 19; Luan S.R./Wikimedia Commons (3.0), p. 8; El Grafico/Wikimedia Commons, p. 10; AP Photo/Associated Press, pp. 11, 20, 21, 22, 23, 24; Popperfoto/Getty Images, p. 12; AP Photo/dpa, p. 14; AP Photo/PA Photos, p. 15; AP Photo/John Lent, p. 16; AP Photo/Kurt Strumpf, p. 17; AP Photo/Heidtmann, p. 18; AP Photo/Anonymous, pp. 25, 27; PCN Photography/Alamy Stock Photo, p. 26.

Cover: Rolls Press/Popperfoto/Getty Images (foreground); AP Photo/Ray Stubblebine (background).